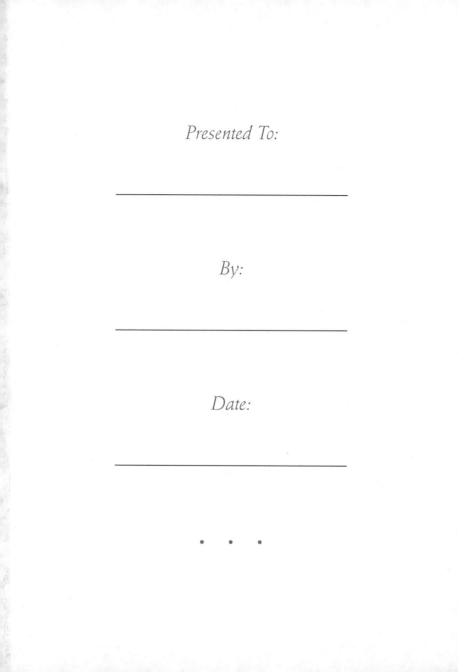

Presented To:

_____

By:

_____

Date:

_____

•   •   •

Everyday Prayers
for
Everyday Cares

f o r   W o m e n

Honor Books
Tulsa, Oklahoma

Everyday Prayers for Everyday Cares for Women
ISBN 1-56292-563-6
Copyright © 2002 by Honor Books
P.O. Box 55388
Tulsa, Oklahoma 74155

Manuscript written by Candy Paull, Nashville, Tennessee.

INTRODUCTION

Women lead busy lives and fill many roles. But regardless of whether they spend their days in the garden or the nursery or the board room, one thing is certain. Their days are often filled with cares, frustrations, and responsibilities.

Everyday Prayers for Everyday Cares for Women is designed to remind you that God is able—able to handle every problem, no matter how great, no matter how seemingly insignificant. The simple prayers and selected scriptures are meant to encourage and uplift you as they urge you to invite God into your day. And the prayers have been placed in categories so that you can find exactly what you need when you need it.

May God richly bless you as you apply these simple prayers to the cares you face each day.

Many women do noble things, but you surpass them all.

PROVERBS 31:29

Contents

When

I FEEL ANGRY . . .

---

*Refrain from anger and turn from wrath; do
not fret—it leads only to evil.*

PSALM 37:8

FATHER,

You help me rule over my anger.

Even when I feel overcome with anger, You are my source of strength and calm. You help me quietly step back and gain a new perspective. Instead of hasty words and angry feelings, You urge me to seek a forgiving heart and an open mind. You teach me not to worry, blame, and play old grudges over and over in my mind. You teach me not to fret over my situation, but instead take positive actions of healing and reconciliation.

Amen.

> *A man's wisdom gives him patience; it is to his glory to overlook an offense.*

PROVERBS 19:11

FATHER,

You give me patience and understanding.

When I feel anger building inside me, I find my refuge and strength in You. You help me to cool off—and give the situation time to resolve, if possible, on its own. You help me see my troubles from a higher perspective. When someone troubles me, You urge me to acknowledge my pain and then move beyond it to offer forgiveness and lovingkindness to the person who has wronged me.

Amen.

Everyone should be quick to listen, slow to speak, and slow to become angry.

JAMES 1: 19

FATHER,

You urge me to listen in spite of my anger.

Right now, my relationships are difficult and painful, and the atmosphere I find myself in seems ready to explode. But I know that You will give me the wisdom to see things clearly, for what they really are. You help me to keep my mouth shut and listen for the truth in what is being said—to read hearts rather than lips. With Your help, I am able to listen with my heart instead of an angry mind.

Amen.

*Better a patient man than a warrior, a man
who controls his temper than one who takes
a city.*

PROVERBS 16:32

FATHER,

You instill in me a quiet heart.

Sometimes I feel lost in a world of power players and win/lose situations, but You give me quiet confidence and a steady heart. You provide inner strength that helps me to remain calm, think clearly, and react with tact and gentleness. You help me to control my temper by showing me a bigger picture—a better way. You teach me that there is no victory in anger and hostility—that victory belongs to those who relinquish their anger to You.

Amen.

•   •   •

When

I FEEL ANXIOUS . . .

Do not be anxious about anything, but in everything, by prayer and petition, with thanksgiving, present your requests to God.

PHILIPPIANS 4:6

FATHER,

You are with me in every situation.

I do not face my troubles alone. I know that, Lord. I can pray to You and find comfort, renewed perception, and wisdom in every circumstance. As I bring my petitions to You, I also have opportunity to give thanks for the gifts You have given me. You've promised to help and guide me. You said You will never leave nor forsake me. I claim Your great promises to me in my time of need. Thank You for Your constant presence in my life.

Amen.

> *How great is your goodness, which you have stored up for those who fear you, which you bestow in the sight of men on those who take refuge in you.*

PSALM 31:19

FATHER,

You are always urging me to place my trust in You.

Right now, I am feeling anxious and I know that I need to draw upon the safety of Your promises. As I reach inside for the seed of faith You have placed in my heart, I thank You, Lord, for giving me the strength to act on that faith and place all my anxious thoughts in Your hands. How wonderful it is to feel Your loving arms around me, comforting me and assuring me that You will never fail me when I trust in Your faithfulness.

Amen.

•   •   •

When

I NEED ASSURANCE . . .

---

*I will lie down and sleep in peace, for you
alone, O LORD, make me dwell in safety.*

PSALM 4:8

FATHER,

You are my place of safety.

Trouble surrounds me, but You are my strong Fortress. When I am fearful, You calm my fears. When I come to You frazzled and afraid, You comfort me and show me that You are a haven—a place of safety. I can sleep in peace, knowing that the morning will bring new vision and hope. In the dark night of my soul, You are my Light and my Salvation. You fill my heart with assurance as I put my hand in Yours.

Amen.

> *"In this world you will have trouble. But take heart! I have overcome the world."*

JOHN 16:33

FATHER,

You have overcome the world.

Today I feel small and powerless, unimportant in the grand scheme of a busy and noisy world. But You remind me that You have overcome the world. Though I have troubles, You are with me in every situation. I can always depend on You, for in Your eyes the world, which seems so fearsome and overwhelming to me, has no real power over me. I am surrounded by Your love. I am victorious in You.

Amen.

• • •

When

I NEED HELP WITH
MY CHILDREN . . .

The promise is for you and your children and for all who are far off—for all whom the Lord our God will call.

ACTS 2:39

FATHER,

You love my children even more than I do.

Here I am again, fretting and worrying over my children. Help me to remember that You also love them. And Your love, Your discipline, Your care is perfect and complete. You always know exactly what they need, and You are never too busy to listen when they come to You with their hopes and dreams. Teach me to love my children as You love them.

Amen.

May the LORD make you increase, both you and your children. May you be blessed by the LORD, the Maker of heaven and earth.

PSALM 115:14-15

FATHER,

You bless and guide my children.

Your Word says that children are a blessing from You. I count my blessings and thank You for each of the children You have given me. I trust that You are blessing them as well, comforting and guiding and protecting them, even when I cannot. I thank You that no matter how troubled they may be, or how far they seem to wander, You will be with them and lead them home. I can trust You to bless my children at all times.

Amen.

•   •   •

When

I NEED COMFORT . . .

"Do not let your hearts be troubled. Trust in God; trust also in me."

JOHN 14:1

FATHER,

When I am troubled, You open Your arms to me.

The storms of life are threatening to destroy my peace. Therefore, I turn to You for strength and comfort. Your everlasting arms are always around me, protecting and guiding me. When my heart is troubled, You shower me with Your tender love. I find solace in Your promises and hope as I worship in Your holy presence. Thank You for calming my fears and offering me the wisdom I need to trust You fully.

Amen.

As a mother comforts her child, so will I comfort you.

ISAIAH 66:13

FATHER,

I am comforted by your love and compassion.

Just now, I feel Your love and compassion wash over me. It is always there, no matter what I have done or left undone. When I come before You with a repentant heart, You are always patient and forgiving, bringing peace to my troubled soul. How grateful I am that You are there for me when I need You most. Your tenderness and love bring relief even in the midst of my darkest night.

Amen.

> *From the fullness of his grace we have all received one blessing after another.*

JOHN 1:16

FATHER,

Your grace is sufficient for me.

In the midst of my heartache and trouble, I know I can come to You and find mercy. You do not belittle or send me away empty handed. Instead, You gently take me in Your arms and comfort me with words of love and encouragement. You remind me that You also suffered, and therefore You know how I feel. I sense Your grace surrounding me and Your mighty arm upholding me. Your grace is more than enough.

Amen.

Cast all your anxiety on him because he cares for you.

1 PETER 5:7

FATHER,

You love me with an everlasting love.

Today, I seem determined to feel sorry for myself and focus on my own problems. But You come quietly before me, urging me to abandon the burden of my fears, worries, and anxieties to You. You allow me to dwell in the comfort of Your promises and bask in the fullness of Your love. You remind me that no matter what I face in life, You will be standing right beside me, lifting me up and comforting me with Your presence.

Amen.

•　•　•

When

I NEED YOUR HELP
AMIDST CONFLICT . . .

Then Peter began to speak, "I now realize how true it is that God does not show favoritism, but accepts men from every nation who fear him and do what is right.

ACTS 10:34-35

FATHER,

You are an impartial and just God.

The conflict I am involved in right now makes me feel hurt, angry, and offended. But I know in my heart, that my emotions will not lead me to a solution—but my faith will. Thank You for helping me to find grace and strength and forgiveness, wisdom and understanding and council in the midst of this situation. I look to You to show me a way of escape, a road to reconciliation.

Amen.

To do what is right and just is more acceptable to the LORD than sacrifice.

PROVERBS 21:3

FATHER,

You are a God of truth and wholeness.

Thank You for reminding me that the conflict that surrounds me is not about who is right or who is wrong. It is about "truth." Though I long for resolution, I also know that I may need to make a stand for the truth. Before I do, I ask You to search my heart and help me to address any deceitfulness that dwells within me. Then I ask that You show me Your path and help me make healing choices for this situation.

Amen.

* * *

When

I AM CONFUSED . . .

Blessed is the man who finds wisdom, the man who gains understanding.

PROVERBS 3:13

FATHER,

You give me wisdom and understanding.

Though I am confused, You bring me clarity. You take my hand during times of change, trouble, and conflict. Walk with me now. Help me to find soundness of mind in spite of my surroundings and my circumstances. Open Your bounty of wisdom and understanding to me so that I can make right choices. And keep me on the straight path, until the skies clear and I can once again see the road before me.

Amen.

> *"I will give you words and wisdom that none of your adversaries will be able to resist or contradict."*

FATHER,

You show me the truth in complex situations.

Though my situation seems blurred and I can see no clear-cut answers or simple solutions, You are there to faithfully point me in the right direction. As I look to You, I receive the benefit of Your wisdom and council. Only then can I find the truth in the midst of my circumstances. As I place my trust in You, I ask that Your Holy Spirit would speak to me and guide me. Thank You for a clear mind and a clean heart, with which to find my way.

Amen.

•   •   •

Everyday Prayers for Everyday Cares for Women • 25

When

I LONG FOR CONTENTMENT . . .

I have learned to be content whatever the circumstances.

PHILIPPIANS 4:11

FATHER,

I find my contentment in You.

You are my Peace, Lord. You are my Source of true joy. When I am frustrated, struggling with the circumstances of life, You come to me, still my restless spirit, and take time to listen. Only a few moments in Your presence reminds me that I have all I need. Your love and care are more than enough. Thank You for providing all I need to live a peaceful and contented life.

Amen.

The fruit of the Spirit is love, joy, peace, longsuffering, gentleness, goodness, faith, Meekness, temperance: against such there is no law.

GALATIANS 5:22 KJV

FATHER,

You fill my heart with the fruit of Your Spirit.

Today I am busy feeling sorry for myself—certain that I am missing out on something. Then I remember all the gifts that You have given me. Love. Joy. Peace. Faith. These are just a part of Your magnificent provision. You fill my life with blessing—the blessing of Your presence, and You promise to walk with me in the midst of every circumstance. Because of You, I can say that "it is well with my soul."

Amen.

*O LORD our Lord, how excellent is thy name
in all the earth! who hast set thy glory above
the heavens.*

PSALM 8:1 KJV

FATHER,

Your gifts are priceless.

Sometimes it seems that everything has a price tag and everyone is weighed and measured by the amount of money they control. But then You remind me that You are the Owner of the rose, the daffodil, and the star-filled sky. And because I am Your child, these priceless creations belong to me as well. How rich I feel when I consider what You have given me.

Amen.

Make it your ambition to lead a quiet life, to mind your own business, and to work with your hands, just as we told you.

1 THESSALONIANS 4:11

FATHER,

You teach me to appreciate quiet pleasures.

Today I find myself looking around and longing for power, prestige, and the fleeting satisfaction of earthly possessions. But You lead me away from selfish ambition and teach me to treasure simplicity and quietness. You encourage me to follow my dreams by submitting them to You and following Your direction. You remind me that hard work is better, easier than striving and pushing my way to the top. You fix my heart on You and set a straight path before me.

Amen.

• • •

When

I NEED COURAGE . . .

Be strong and courageous. Do not be afraid or terrified because of them, for the LORD your God goes with you; he will never leave you nor forsake you.

DEUTERONOMY 31:6

FATHER,

You give me the courage to deal with my circumstances.

This challenge I'm facing in my life makes me feel alone, but I know that You are by my side. I listen for Your gentle words—and they are there, encouraging me to confront my fears, face my circumstances. Without You, I know that I would not have the courage I need to stand my ground. I would be overwhelmed in the midst of my situation. Instead, I will look to You for courage and strength. *Amen.*

Fear of man will prove to be a snare, but whoever trusts in the LORD is kept safe.

PROVERBS 29:25

FATHER,

You take away my fear.

Today, I feel threatened, afraid, because of a certain person and situation. Thank You for tenderly reminding me that You are right beside me, providing me with Your strength and courage. No matter what happens—even if I should lose my earthly life—You will never leave me. You will stand beside me every step of the way. Because You are with me, I will not fear what man can do to me.

Amen.

> *You are my hiding place; you will protect me from trouble and surround me with songs of deliverance.*

PSALM 32:7

FATHER,

You are my hiding place.

When I am afraid, I come to You. When I must be courageous for others, You give me Your strength. You protect and surround me with angels. When I feel weak, I find shelter in Your mighty arms. Though I may not be able to express my fears outwardly to others, You know all my thoughts completely. Thank You for surrounding me with Your love and giving me a safe place in the midst of trouble.

Amen.

The LORD is with me; I will not be afraid.
What can man do to me?

PSALM 118:6

FATHER,

You give me confidence.

Right now, my obstacles and adversaries appear larger than life. I feel so small in the presence of my enemies. But when I come to You, I see another perspective. You remind me that no obstacle, living or dead, is able to keep You from accomplishing Your purposes in my life. You remind me that You are the God who helped David slay Goliath, and You will give me courage to slay the giants in my life as well.

Amen.

•   •   •

When

I FEAR DEATH . . .

---

*I am convinced that neither death nor life,
neither angels nor demons, neither the present
nor the future, nor any powers, neither height
nor depth, nor anything else in all creation will
be able to separate us from the love of God
that is in Christ Jesus our Lord.*

ROMANS 8:38-39

FATHER,

Death cannot separate me from Your love.

I know that death is the final enemy—one which You
have vanquished. Though I do not understand the pain and
suffering I see in this world, I set my heart free to take hold
of Your promise of eternal life. Your Son came to carry the
debt of my sin and guarantee to me that even death—the
final enemy—cannot separate me from Your love.

Amen.

Our God is a God who saves; from the
Sovereign LORD comes escape from death.

PSALM 68:20

FATHER,

You are the God who saves me.

Though I am walking through the valley of the shadow of death, You are with me. I can safely place my trust in You because You have faced death on Your own terms and conquered it. Your victory purchased for me the promise of new life in Your heavenly Kingdom—eternal life. Thank You for taking away the sting of death and replacing it with the promise of life everlasting.

Amen.

When the perishable has been clothed with the imperishable, and the mortal with immortality, then the saying that is written will come true: "Death has been swallowed up in victory."

1 CORINTHIANS 15:54

FATHER,

The victory is Yours.

You are a great and glorious God who is victorious over death. Your resurrected Son has paved the way for a great procession of life. Decay and destruction will be transformed one day into flowering, fruitful life. I thank You that one day this body I live in will be transformed, and I shall live on the other side of earthly death—triumphant forever. It is in this hope that I rest.

Amen.

Jesus said to her, "I am the resurrection and the life. He who believes in me will live, even though he dies; and whoever lives and believes in me will never die. Do you believe this?"

JOHN 11:25-26

FATHER,

You are the Resurrection and the Life.

The mystery of death and resurrection are beyond my understanding. But Your promises are clear—You are my life. When I am grieving the loss of someone I love, You remind me that death means only a temporary separation. One bright day, there will be a reunion in Your heavenly Kingdom—a reunion that will never end. Thank You for Your reassurance that death is not the end, but a beginning in You.

Amen.

• • •

When

I FEEL DEPRESSED . . .

*Ask where the good way is and walk in it,
and you will find rest for your souls.*

JEREMIAH 6:16

FATHER,

You comfort and encourage me.

Today I am depressed, and it seems that nothing I do can make me feel better. I dwell in dark and gloomy thoughts, rehearsing the worst case scenarios over and over. You ask me to let go of anxious thoughts and allow myself to be comforted. You promise me rest and refreshing in Your presence. Thank You for the assurance that even my own thoughts cannot separate me from Your love and care.

Amen.

The LORD is close to the brokenhearted and saves those who are crushed in spirit.

PSALM 34:18

FATHER,

You understand my sadness.

Life has its sorrow and tears as well as its gladness and laughter. But no matter how sad I may feel, You remind me to look up into Your accepting eyes and rejoice in the fact that I am Your child and nothing can take me out of Your hand or separate me from Your presence. Your gentle words give me hope that the dark night of my soul will soon end and before me will dawn a glorious new day.

Amen.

> *Why are you downcast, O my soul? Why so disturbed within me? Put your hope in God, for I will yet praise him, my Savior and my God.*

PSALM 42:5

FATHER,

I will praise You even when I am sad.

Thank You for reminding me that depression does not have to defeat me. I do not have to live in sadness and despair. I can choose to light a candle and worship You. I can choose to praise You even in my pain, believing that one day, choosing to praise You will lead me into a time of joy and renewal. Through my tears, I look to You and see a rainbow of hope.

Amen.

My comfort in my suffering is this: Your promise preserves my life.

PSALM 119:50

FATHER,

You renew my life.

Though depression has come over me like a heavy cloud, I know that behind the cloud the rays of Your love still shine. I comfort myself with the many promises You have given. I reassure my doubting mind with the knowledge that as spring follows winter, so joy will come after a time of sorrow. You renew my life in mysterious and glorious ways. I wait for Your perfect timing.

Amen.

*   *   *

When

I STRUGGLE WITH DISAPPOINTMENT . . .

Hope deferred makes the heart sick, but a longing fulfilled is a tree of life.

PROVERBS 13:12

FATHER,

You are my Hope when life lets me down.

Today I am discouraged because projects, plans, and dreams have not come together as I planned. I feel sad and my days feel like a weary march across an endless desert. But then, You remind me that You were with the children of Israel as they wandered in the desert—and You brought them to the promised land. I grieve my disappointments, but I put my trust in Your promises of deliverance.

Amen.

No matter how many promises God has made, they are "Yes" in Christ.

2 CORINTHIANS 1:20

FATHER,

You love to say "yes" to Your children.

I feel like a disappointed child, denied some pleasure. Forgive me, Lord, and help me to remember that You are a loving Father who wants to give good gifts to all of His children. Just as a father makes wise decisions for a child's highest good, so You make wise decisions for my highest good. I choose to believe Your promises and that this disappointment is part of a greater plan being worked out on my behalf. Thank You for assuring me that this "no" will lead me to a better "yes".

Amen.

•   •   •

When

I NEED DISCIPLINE . . .

Brothers, stop thinking like children. In regard to evil be infants, but in your thinking be adults.

1 CORINTHIANS 14:20

FATHER,

As I grow in You, I become more disciplined.

Like everyone else, I have developed a need for instant gratification. But in Your love, You remind me that I have been called to be childlike rather than childish. You teach me to patiently wait for a fruitful harvest. You help me to mature in my thinking and learn the discipline of an artist or athlete, working toward a worthy goal. Thank You for calling me to maturity.

Amen.

> *"Come unto me, all ye that labour and are heavy laden, and I will give you rest."*

MATTHEW 11:28 KJV

FATHER,

You lighten my load and help me.

You walk with me, a fellow "yoke mate" who carries my burden. When I struggle, You are there beside me, lifting the weight off my shoulders. When I am discouraged, You encourage me to keep on keeping on. Your discipline is not one of rules and regulations, but of love and patience. Because You love me and believe in me, I find new strength to stay my course.

Amen.

•   •   •

When

I Am Discouraged . . .

Hope does not disappoint us, because God has poured out his love into our hearts by the Holy Spirit, whom he has given us.

ROMANS 5:5

FATHER,

You lay before me an eternal perspective.

I am so grateful, Lord, that even when I can see only part of my situation, You see the whole picture. When I stop focusing on my circumstances but instead focus on You, I discover a higher perspective. I let go of my own timing and agendas, opening myself to Your perfect will. Thank You for Your promise to work all things together for my good if I place my hope in You.

Amen.

> *They cried to the LORD in their trouble, and he saved them from their distress.*

PSALM 107:13

FATHER,

You answer my cry for help.

I just want to thank You, Lord. In times of trouble, You are my Glory and the Lifter of my head. When I am between a rock and a hard place, You are my Rescuer. When I find myself boxed in by my own fear, You open the door and set me free. Thank You for Your gentle reminder that You are always here beside me, helping me, guiding me. My trust is in You, Lord. I will stand still and see the deliverance You will bring to my circumstances.

Amen.

* * *

When

I AM DOUBTFUL . . .

Dear friends, build yourselves up in your most holy faith, and pray in the Holy Spirit.

JUDE 20

FATHER,

You are the focus of my faith.

Doubt is assailing me and whispering in my ear, but I will focus my thoughts on You, Lord. When doubt tells me things will never change and You have deserted me, I meditate on Your promises. Thank You for increasing my faith to meet the challenge that doubt presents. Help me to root myself even deeper in You and ground myself in Your Word, so that I can overcome my doubts, not with arguments, but with wisdom and understanding.

Amen.

> *I was young and now I am old, yet I have never seen the righteous forsaken or their children begging bread.*

FATHER,

I know You will never forsake me.

Right now, I feel lonely, yet I am not alone. You are here with me. You do not abandon me as a punishment for my doubting. Instead, You give me reassurance that You are always working on my behalf, preparing the way and bringing me exactly what I need. Your faithfulness teaches me to wait patiently for You. Thank You for taking my doubts and replacing them with faith, hope, and love.

Amen.

•   •   •

When

I NEED ENCOURAGEMENT . . .

I am the LORD, your God, who takes hold of your right hand and says to you, Do not fear; I will help you.

ISAIAH 41:13

FATHER,

You are my Help and Encouragement.

Life has beaten me up and I am hurting, but still I choose to listen to Your gentle voice reassuring me of Your love and care. You open my eyes to see all the abundant graces You have placed in my life. You heal my hurting soul and set me back on my feet. Your Spirit encourages me from within, singing songs of healing. Thank You for always knowing what I need most.

Amen.

The LORD delights in those who fear him, who put their hope in his unfailing love.

FATHER,

You are my Encourager.

The realities of life have thrown my plans into disarray, and I am tempted to give myself to discouragement and frustration. But You are always there to strengthen my weak knees and help me stand my ground. You remind me of my blessings—all the wonderful gifts You have placed in my life. And You urge me to submit my plans to You so that they might succeed.

Amen.

*   *   *

When

I NEED ENDURANCE . . .

Thou therefore endure hardness, as a good soldier of Jesus Christ.

2 TIMOTHY 2:3 KJV

FATHER,

I give my gifts and talents to You.

Sometimes I wonder if my dreams will ever come to pass. I begin to doubt that my future is still safely held in the palm of Your hand. Then I hear Your voice, reminding me that Your plans for me will never fail— they are secure within Your perfect will for my life. And You urge me to remain strong in my resolve, all the while trusting in You and Your faithfulness until my dreams are realized.

Amen.

My dear brothers, stand firm. Let nothing move you.

1 CORINTHIANS 15:58

FATHER,

You give me the power to stand firm.

Today I'm tempted to give up. But You are there, urging me to stand firm. You give me the strength to endure hard times and come through victorious. Thank You, Lord, that my triumphs don't depend entirely on me, for if they did, I would never reach the mark. With You helping me though, I know I can remain strong, pushing forward until I reach the goal.

Amen.

•   •   •

When

I FEEL LIKE A FAILURE . . .

If our heart condemn us, God is greater than our heart, and knoweth all things.

1 JOHN 3:20 KJV

FATHER,

You do not condemn me.

Today it seems that I just can't measure up to expectations—my own or anyone else's. I call myself a failure and put a big sign on myself that says "not good enough." But You never condemn me or call me a failure. You know my sin, but You cover it with Your blood. You know my weakness, but You uphold me with Your strength. You replace the words on the sign with "made perfect in My strength." You set me free.

Amen.

The foolishness of God is wiser than man's wisdom, and the weakness of God is stronger than man's strength.

1 CORINTHIANS 1:25

FATHER,

You redefine failure by redefining success.

Today I got caught up in the world's definition of success. I began to measure myself by those around me. Thank You for reminding me, Lord, that Kingdom success is not a game of "one-up-manship." It is based solely on living a life that is pleasing in Your sight. I am never a failure as long as I am looking to You to guide my steps and illumine my path.

Amen.

•   •   •

When

I LONG TO HAVE
MORE FAITH . . .

*The only thing that counts is faith expressing
itself through love.*

GALATIANS 5:6

FATHER,

You teach me how to live by faith.

I have been so busy intellectualizing my faith that I forget how faith grows in simple action. What good is it to believe the right doctrine but ignore the needs of those whom You have placed in my life? Today I express my love for You through faithful action. A cup of cold water, an encouraging word, a gift of my time and energy—each act of love becomes a catalyst for my faith.

Amen.

Take up the shield of faith, with which you can extinguish all the flaming arrows of the evil one.

EPHESIANS 6:16

FATHER,

Your Word is my source of faith.

When my faith is weak, I meditate on Your Word. I read the stories of the people who found faith in Your presence as they encountered the extremities of life. Help me, Lord, to nurture my faith with Scripture and prayer. Remind me to dress myself each day in Your Word, trusting that I will find the strength and assurance I need to walk by faith and accomplish Your perfect will for my life.

Amen.

Without faith it is impossible to please God, because anyone who comes to him must believe that he exists and that he rewards those who earnestly seek him.

HEBREWS 11:6

FATHER,

You are pleased when I live by faith.

I've been making my life complicated again, Lord. I have been trying to pull myself up by my bootstraps, trying to live my life without You. I get so caught up in "being good" and having the "right" answers that I forget it is not through my work, but by Your Spirit, that my success is ensured. Thank You, Lord, for giving me a heart of repentance and setting my feet back upon the right path.

Amen.

Trust in the LORD with all your heart and lean not on your own understanding.

PROVERBS 3:5

FATHER,

I trust in You today.

I am not alone. You are with me. You have always been with me, even when I did not know it. Today I come once again, acknowledging that I have not trusted You with my whole heart. I give my heart to You, believing that You will give me enough faith for today's needs. Though Your ways are mysterious, they are kind and You reward my childlike faith.

Amen.

* * *

When

I FEEL FEARFUL . . .

The LORD is good, a refuge in times of trouble.
He cares for those who trust in him.

NAHUM 1:7

FATHER,

You are my safe Place.

I am troubled and afraid, and I know nothing else to do but run to Your arms. I bring You my fears, my failures, my inadequacies, and ask You to fill me with Your strength, courage, and faith. You remind me that I am loved. You promise to protect and guide me. I will not fear, for You surround me with Your love and mercy. You sustain me with Your wisdom and truth. I have found a safe hiding place in You.

Amen.

*If you make the Most High your dwelling—
even the LORD, who is my refuge—then no
harm will befall you, no disaster will come
near your tent.*

PSALM 91:9-10

FATHER,

You are my Protector.

I am afraid, but You are here, right by my side, urging me to place my trust in Your promises and leave my fears at Your feet. Even though I cannot see a solution to my problem, I am reminded that You have never forsaken me. You have faithfully cared for me every day of my life. Thank You, Lord, for watching over me and keeping me in the hollow of Your hand.

Amen.

God did not give us a spirit of timidity, but a spirit of power, of love, and of self-discipline.

2 TIMOTHY 1:7

FATHER,

I place my confidence in You.

I feel weak and terrified, but I am so thankful that Your Spirit is there to strengthen and uphold me by reminding me that You have given me Your power to overcome the obstacles I am facing in my life. In the midst of my weakness, You have given me the victory. Thank You for Your hand of mercy that is extended to me that I might conquer my fears and live a victorious life.

Amen.

> *In righteousness you will be established:*
> *Tyranny will be far from you; you will have*
> *nothing to fear. Terror will be far removed; it*
> *will not come near you.*

ISAIAH 54:14

FATHER,

You calm my fears.

Though I am afraid, I feel Your presence deep inside my heart. With my spirit, I can hear You whisper, "Peace. Be still," as the storm rages around me. As I trust and pray and wait on You, I find I am lifted on eagle's wings of faith. Thank You, Lord, for listening to the cry of my heart and ministering to me at the point of my need. I shall praise You all the days of my life.

Amen.

•   •   •

When

I NEED HELP WITH MY FINANCES . . .

A generous man will prosper; he who refreshes others will himself be refreshed.

PROVERBS 11:25

FATHER,

You are a generous God.

Lord, I know that I am called to be like You. You are generous, and You call me to be generous as well. Whether I have much or little, there is always enough to share. Provide an opportunity for me to share today. I promise to listen for Your still, small voice guiding me to that person who needs what I have to give. Thank You for allowing me to bless myself by blessing others.

Amen.

God is able to make all grace abound toward you, so that in all things at all times, having all that you need, you will abound in every good work.

2 CORINTHIANS 9:8

FATHER,

You give me all that I need.

Thank You for showering me with blessings every day—simple things like my daily bread and a bed on which to rest my body. Sometimes I become focused on what I don't have, but when I turn my eyes on You, I am reminded of all that I do have and my heart is filled with gratitude. I know that You will continue to provide all that I need, for You are kind and loving.

Amen.

It is required that those who have been given a trust must prove faithful.

FATHER,

Give me a generous heart like Yours.

You have richly blessed me, Lord. Nevertheless, I find it difficult to share what You have given me with others. Open my heart and open my hands. Show me how to enrich myself while enriching others. And thank You for revealing to me that the difficulties I'm now experiencing are a result of my own lack of generosity. As I follow Your principle of giving, I believe You will open up Your windows of blessing to me once more.

Amen.

Each one should use whatever gift he has received to serve others, faithfully administering God's grace in its various forms.

1 PETER 4:10

FATHER,

I honor you with my life.

It's easy enough to give money to help others, but I see that You have called me to give much more—my very life. Open my heart to see how You wish to use the gifts and talents You have placed in my life to serve others. Guide me as I strive to pour out myself. As I learn to walk in paths of service, I believe that You will take care of all my material needs.

Amen.

* * *

When

I NEED TO FORGIVE . . .

---

*When you stand praying, if you hold any-
thing against anyone, forgive him, so that your
Father in heaven may forgive you your sins.*

MARK 11:25

FATHER,

You call me to be merciful.

Forgiving those who have wronged me is not an easy
thing. Instead I find myself wanting to hold a grudge—
give back evil for evil. Thank You for loving me enough
to chasten me when I persist in such negative behaviors.
Thank You for teaching me that forgiveness is the only
way to free my heart from the bondage and destruction
of hatred and anger and revenge. You are a good and
wise God.

Amen.

Bear with each other and forgive whatever grievances you may have against one another. Forgive as the Lord forgave you.

COLOSSIANS 3:13

FATHER,

You forgive me so I can forgive others.

When others hurt and abuse me, I want to strike out at them. But You urge me to forgive. I find that difficult to do until You remind me that I have also been found guilty. Others have suffered at my hands, often without my even knowing it. It is then that I see and understand. I must forgive as freely as I myself have been forgiven. Thank You for covering my transgressions with Your love and the blood of Your precious Son.

Amen.

•   •   •

When

I NEED FORGIVENESS . . .

He forgives all my sins and heals all my diseases.

PSALM 103:3 NLT

FATHER,

You forgive and heal.

I know I have been wrong. And though it has taken me a long time to admit it, I now come to You and ask for forgiveness. I ask You, Lord, to wash me clean, take away my transgression and heal me. For the pain I have caused others, I ask You to show me how I might make recompense. And when that is impossible, I ask You to comfort and console and heal the person I have harmed. Thank You for Your mercy and grace.

Amen.

In him we have redemption through his blood, the forgiveness of sins, in accordance with the riches of God's grace.

EPHESIANS 1:7

FATHER,

Your grace flows to me like a river.

You forgive my sins, even before I ask. It is Your grace that helps me become aware of my sin and my need to ask for Your mercy. Now in this quiet moment, I want to thank You for Your grace. Like a stream bed that has been dry and is now filled with spring rains, so my heart is filled with Your love and kindness. Open my heart to receive even more of You.

Amen.

He saved us, not because of righteous things we had done, but because of his mercy.

TITUS 3:5

FATHER,

You are merciful to Your children.

I am Your child—not because I deserve to be, but because You loved me first and gave Your Son for me. When I stumble, You pick me up. When I fail, You help me start anew. I have a new beginning because of Your love and grace. I ask forgiveness, knowing that You will wash me clean. Thank You for Your mercy, which allows me to lift my head and sing a song of praise.

Amen.

*Because of the Lord's great love we are not con-
sumed, for his compassions never fail. They are
new every morning; great is your faithfulness.*

LAMENTATIONS 3:22-23

FATHER,

Every morning Your mercies are new.

Thank You for making each new day a new beginning.
Even when I fail You, like I did today, You never fail me.
You forgive me and put me back on my feet to live again.
Without Your love and mercy, I would perish for I have
no hope in myself. O great and mighty God, my heart is
singing with gladness and praise for Your lovingkindness
poured out on my life.

Amen.

•　　•　　•

When

I NEED A FRIEND . . .

I no longer call you servants. . . . Instead, I
have called you friends.

JOHN 15:15

FATHER,

You are my Friend.

You are my Father in Heaven, but You have also chosen to call me "friend." As we spend time together, I want only to know You better, to learn what I can do to please You. Your friendship has taught me to reach out to others just as You have reached out to me. Your friendship is constant and faithful. Thank You for opening Your arms of love to me and teaching me what being a friend is all about.

Amen.

I am a friend to all who fear you, to all who follow your precepts.

PSALM 119:63

FATHER,

I find fellowship with Your people.

Today I found myself lonely, longing to have friends. Thank You for reminding me that there are those with whom I have a very special bond. In fact, you urge me to find my friends among Your people. It is with them that friendship takes on another element—we are all part of the same family, Your family. Therefore, we can encourage each other in a spiritual journey through life. Thank You, Lord, for Your wisdom and encouragement.

Amen.

As iron sharpens iron, so one man sharpens another.

PROVERBS 27:17

FATHER,

My friends teach me about You and about myself.

I'm so frustrated—I hate being in conflict with a friend. But today, we just seemed to rub each another the wrong way. Help me step back and see what is happening from a higher perspective. My friends often teach me things that I can learn in no other way. I thank You for faithful friends who are willing to tell me difficult truths, who forgive me when I need forgiveness, and who have been faithful through difficult times.

Amen.

"Greater love has no one than this, that he lay down his life for his friends."

JOHN 15:13

FATHER,

You help me to be a good friend.

Continue to teach me by Your example that friendship requires love, attention, and an open heart. Open my heart to love others more fully, reaching out to others and nurturing the long-term friendships You have placed in my life. You are the greatest Friend of all and therefore, I know I can trust You to guide me as I learn to be a better friend to those You have placed in my life.

Amen.

*   *   *

When

I AM FRUSTRATED . . .

He will have no fear of bad news; his heart is steadfast, trusting in the LORD.

PSALM 112:7

FATHER,

I can trust my troubles to You.

Bad news, detours, plans that misfire, troubles large and small—sometimes it seems they come in waves to frustrate and defeat my dreams. During this difficult time, I am reminded to trust in You. I do not know how the problems will be resolved, but Your assurance allows me to wait as You work all things together for good. Thank You, Lord, for all Your ways are faithful and true.

Amen.

> *We say with confidence, "The Lord is my*
> *helper; I will not be afraid. What can man do*
> *to me?"*

HEBREWS 13:6

FATHER,

You give me quiet confidence.

Though I am frustrated by life, You calm my fears. You remind me to meditate on Your promises and to remember all the times You have brought me through my troubles. You have taught me that anger is futile and takes the joy from my life. Therefore, I will trust You today and wait for the quiet confidence and peace You always send to fill my heart and heal me.

Amen.

Cast all your anxiety on him because he cares for you.

1 PETER 5:7

FATHER,

You calm my spirit.

No matter what is bothering me—a missed deadline, a traffic jam, an argument with my spouse, a financial situation, a sick child who won't stop crying, a friend who has let me down—no matter what—You are always there to ease my troubled mind and help me deal with the crisis. Thank You, Lord, for giving me the confidence that no matter how many frustrations pile up, You will always give me the strength and stamina to handle them. *Amen.*

I will instruct you and teach you in the way you should go; I will counsel you and watch over you.

PSALM 32:8

FATHER,

You give me wisdom and patience.

When I am frustrated, it is easy to say the wrong thing. It is easy to criticize, to blame, to take out my anger on someone else. Sometimes hidden thoughts will come to the surface and I'll blurt out ugly words in spite of myself. I ask Your help to hold my tongue during this frustrating situation. May Your peace fill my spirit so that the beauty of patience and discretion may shine through me.

Amen.

•   •   •

When

I AM SEARCHING FOR
FULFILLMENT . . .

---

*Planted in the house of the LORD, they will flour-
ish in the courts of our God. They will still bear
fruit in old age, they will stay fresh and green.*

PSALM 92:13-14

FATHER,

I send my roots deep in Your love.

I love you, Father. I come to You, knowing that I will find rest in Your presence. You are my Hope and my Salvation. When I am looking for what gives my life meaning, You are the Answer. My restless, yearning heart will find no peace until it finds You. You are the One who renews me and enables me to flourish and grow, fulfilling Your every purpose for my life.

Amen.

We pray this in order that you may live a life worthy of the Lord and may please him in every way: bearing fruit in every good work, growing in the knowledge of God.

COLOSSIANS 1:10

FATHER,

You are my Fulfillment.

I used to search for fulfillment. I was sure it could be found in earthly possessions, careers, friends, and family. Those things do provide a temporary sense of fulfillment. But nothing gives me lasting fulfillment like my relationship with You. Restore my patience to seek the highest good in my situation. Restore my courage to dream and my ability to persevere until my dreams come true.

Amen.

Still other seed fell on good soil, where it produced a crop—a hundred, sixty, or thirty times what was sown.

MATTHEW 13:8

FATHER,

You bring my hopes and dreams to pass.

As I choose to live in Your will and continue to plant the good seed of faith in the soil of my life, I know that You are giving me favor and leading me in the ways of success. As a farmer patiently waters, weeds, and waits for the seed to grow, so I wait for You to bring my dreams to realization. I thank You that even as I wait for fulfillment, You promise my time will one day come.

Amen.

He is like a tree planted by streams of water,
which yields its fruit in season and whose leaf
does not wither. Whatever he does prospers.

PSALM 1:3

FATHER,

You nourish my spirit.

Thank You for all the good gifts You have given to me. In this season, when my dreams have not yet come true, remind me to count the blessings I already enjoy. As I count my blessings, help me to realize that I am already rich in You. Show me that You are refining my dreams, preparing me to receive even greater gifts in due season because I trust in You.

Amen.

• • •

When

I AM GRIEVING . . .

Do not grieve, for the joy of the LORD is your strength.

NEHEMIAH 8:10

FATHER,

You bring me joy even in sorrow.

In times of sadness, You are my Comfort. Though I am grieving, I know that the losses I sustain in this life are not the end of the story. As Christ was resurrected after His death, so I know that those I have lost will one day be found as I meet them again in heaven. I trust that Your love will strengthen me and that a rainbow of hope will shine through my tears. Thank You, Lord, for a future hope that cannot be disappointed.

Amen.

He was . . . a man of sorrows, and familiar with suffering. . . . Surely he took up our infirmities and carried our sorrows.

FATHER,

You do not leave me alone in my grief.

Grief is a lonely business, but I am not alone in my sorrow. You are with me. You understand my grief because You also lost a loved one to death—Your very own Son. And You remind me that Your Son was resurrected and returned to You. One day my loved one will also be resurrected in Your heavenly Kingdom and we will be reunited in a place where there will never again be sorrow or weeping. Thank you, Lord, for the gift of eternal life.

Amen.

Everyday Prayers for Everyday Cares for Women • 87

"Do not be afraid, little flock, for your Father has been pleased to give you the kingdom."

LUKE 12:32

FATHER,

The kingdom, the power, and the glory are Yours.

You are the sovereign God. You reign in power and have power over death and hell. You are the merciful God, the One who weeps with those who weep. You promise that one day my sorrow will be turned to joy. Though weeping may endure for a night, joy comes in the morning. You are the God of resurrection and power. Thank You for holding my hand through this difficult time.

Amen.

The ransomed of the LORD will return. They will enter Zion with singing: everlasting joy will crown their heads. Gladness and joy will overtake them, and sorrow and sighing will flee away.

ISAIAH 51:11

FATHER,

You are my eternal Joy.

One day the sorrow and suffering of this earthly life will be over. I comfort myself with Your promise of eternal joy. I am Your child, and You guide me gently on my pilgrimage through this world. But You also remind me that my true home is with You, where the saints shall rejoice forever in Your love. Help me to keep my eyes focused on eternal realities.

Amen.

•   •   •

When

I NEED GUIDANCE . . .

*He guides the humble in what is right and
teaches them his way.*

PSALM 25:9

FATHER,

You promise to guide me.

You order my steps and guide me in the way I should go. You teach me Your ways and pick me up when I stumble. Your Word is like a lantern guiding my feet one step at a time down the path of life. Thank You, Lord, for providing the answer I need and showing me which way to turn. I praise You for being my trustworthy Guide and Helper.

Amen.

Guide me in your truth and teach me, for you are God my Savior, and my hope is in you all day long.

PSALM 25:5

FATHER,

I trust You through each day.

Every day I have a choice. I can choose to lean on my own understanding, or I can choose to trust You. Sometimes You speak through my common sense understanding. Sometimes You teach me to walk by faith and not by sight. Regardless of my situation, I will listen every day for Your guidance in my life. Thank You, Lord, for faithfully walking beside me all the way.

Amen.

> *When he, the Spirit of truth, comes, he will guide you into all truth.*

JOHN 16:13

FATHER,

You help me to discern the truth.

This situation I am facing seems so ambiguous and I am not sure what to believe, but You urge me to trust Your guidance. My intuition is a gift that tells me when a situation is dangerous, even though it might look safe. Thank You, Lord, for teaching me to trust my intuition and for leading me to safety in my current situation. I will listen carefully to Your Spirit and look to You for guidance.

Amen.

*I will lead the blind by ways they have not
known, along unfamiliar paths I will guide
them; I will turn the darkness into light before
them and make the rough places smooth.*

ISAIAH 42:16

FATHER,

You are a trustworthy Guide.

What would I do without You, Lord. You answer
before I call. You guide me even when I do not know I
am being guided. Circumstances arrange themselves
without my needing to manipulate them. Help comes
from unexpected sources. When I travel with You, even
the unknown places are safer than a known way. Thank
You for guiding me through my current situation and
opening and closing doors before me.

Amen.

* * *

When

I AM SEARCHING FOR HAPPINESS . . .

Go and enjoy choice food and sweet drinks, and send some to those who have nothing prepared. This day is sacred to our Lord.

NEHEMIAH 8:10

FATHER,

You teach me to seek happiness in the small pleasures.

You have shown me, Lord, that every day is sacred to You, filled with small pleasures that bring joy and happiness to my life. I will see them if I am faithful to pause and look for them—a bird singing in the tree outside my window, a rose in full bloom, a child at play, and so much more. I am surrounded by countless blessings, gifts of love from Your hand. I'm so grateful for Your goodness to me.

Amen.

> *"I have told you this so that my joy may be in you and that your joy may be complete."*

JOHN 15:11

FATHER,

I find true happiness in You.

You have taught me that I once longed for a happiness completely dependent on circumstances. But now I know that true and lasting happiness flows from my relationship with You. As I spend time with You, my heart is gladdened. You make me happy from the inside out. And that allows me to live in an attitude of happiness rather than a feeling that comes and goes. Thank You for this wonderful gift.

Amen.

You have made known to me the path of life;
you will fill me with joy in your presence, with
eternal pleasures at your right hand.

PSALM 16:11

FATHER,

You are my Joy-Giver and my Happiness-Maker.

I see so many people running around trying to find happiness in possessions, status, and popularity. And I catch myself doing the same thing—running after things that can never satisfy me. To be honest, I'm still tempted by those things at times. Remind me often, Lord, that true happiness flows from inside me and is a product of my relationship with You.

Amen.

Those who sow in tears will reap with songs of joy.

PSALM 126:5

FATHER,

You remind me that happiness sometimes comes after tears.

Today, Lord, sadness seems to be following behind me. I can't stop the tears, and happiness seems to have taken a vacation from my life. I struggle to lift my head before You. But You always seem to understand my darker moods, and when I offer them to You, I feel Your gentle hand pushing away the clouds and opening my soul to the sunshine of Your love.

Amen.

*   *   *

When

I NEED HEALING . . .

He forgives all my sins and heals all my diseases.

PSALM 103:3 NLT

FATHER,

You are my Healer.

Today sickness has entered my life, and my body is wracked with pain. But it is such a comfort to know that You are with me. I can rest in the knowledge that my physical health is of great concern to You, for You have said so in Your Word. As I look to You for healing, I am glad to know that the answer is already on the way. You are a good Father who watches over every aspect of my well being.

Amen.

> *"According to your faith will it be done to you."*

MATTHEW 9:29

FATHER,

You are my Source of faith.

Lord, I am trying to believe—help my unbelief! Help me to take hold of the provision You made for me on the cross when You took on Yourself all my sicknesses and diseases. You carried them so that I could be healed and live a life of health and wholeness. I know what You have done for me, but I need to *know* it with my heart. Quicken my spirit, Lord, that I might receive Your gracious provision.

Amen.

By his wounds we are healed.

ISAIAH 53:5

FATHER,

You heal me.

Sometimes, Lord, I wonder about suffering. I wonder why some are healed but others are not. I know from Your Word that it is Your intention for all Your children to live in health. Therefore, I choose to trust You when healing is evident. And I also trust You when it is not. I trust You when I understand and when I do not. I trust You because I will never be disappointed when I place my trust in You.

Amen.

He asked him, "Do you want to get well?"

JOHN 5:6

FATHER,

I want to walk in health and wholeness.

Thank You, Lord, for Your sacrifice that makes it possible for me to choose to be healed. As I exercise my faith during this time of sickness, I ask that You would heal my body and return it to wholeness. I also ask that You would heal my soul and my mind at the same time that I might walk in the fullness of Your provision for my life.

Amen.

* * *

When

I Need Help . . .

> *The LORD is my strength and my shield; my heart trusts in him, and I am helped.*
>
> PSALM 28:7

FATHER,

You are my Help and my Salvation.

Thank You for the wonderful gifts You have given me. You have provided me with abundant blessings and the help I need. You have never let me down. Today, when I need Your help once again, there is no shame in asking. It is my joy to come to You with my needs and Your delight to provide for each need with wisdom and love.

Amen.

> *We say with confidence, "The Lord is my helper; I will not be afraid. What can man do to me?"*

HEBREWS 13:6

FATHER,

You are the Source of my confident faith.

In every situation, You are my Provider and Protector. In every relationship, You are my Peacemaker. You guide me all of the time, wherever I go, helping me to navigate each obstacle as it appears in my path. You are totally trustworthy and will never let me down. Because I depend on You, I am confident that help will come at exactly the right time.

Amen.

I will go before you and will level the mountains; I will break down gates of bronze and cut through bars of iron.

ISAIAH 45:2

FATHER,

I rest in the flow of Your will.

Lord, You parted the Red Sea and freed the children of Israel. You lead us on life's pilgrimage, opening the way before us in mysterious and sometimes miraculous ways. I have been faithful, striving to do my best in this situation. Now I turn the situation over to You and release my expectations, trusting in Your deliverance. I wait for Your intervention in my troublesome affairs and thank You for the power of Your ways in my life.

Amen.

Do not fear, for I am with you; do not be dismayed, for I am your God. I will strengthen you and help you, I will uphold you with my righteous right hand.

ISAIAH 41:10

FATHER,

You are present in times of trouble.

Even now, in this turbulent situation, You are with me, sustaining me. Though I don't know how You will bring resolution to my problem, I rest in Your promise to bring good from every circumstance in my life. You are my Hope and my Salvation. You have always helped me in the past, and today is no different. You draw near to me as I draw near to You.

Amen.

•   •   •

When

I NEED HOPE . . .

Everything that was written in the past was written to teach us, so that through endurance and the encouragement of the Scriptures we might have hope.

ROMANS 15:4

FATHER,

You are my Source of hope.

Thank You, Lord, for helping me to find hope in the pages of the Bible and the wise observations of friends. I find hope in the books I read, the songs I listen to, and the stories I hear. But each of these good things that speak hope to me are from You—so many wonderful ways in which to experience Your hope. Every source of hope finds its beginning in You.

Amen.

> *When calamity comes, the wicked are brought down, but even in death the righteous have a refuge.*

PROVERBS 14:32

FATHER,

You are my Refuge and my Hope.

Today, I am tempted to doubt, allowing despair to overwhelm me in a giant wave of grief. But instead, I turn to You. You are my Refuge in stormy times. Even death cannot separate me from You. You are my Hope and the Sanctuary I run to when I cannot withstand the fury of the storm. Like a hidden cave deep in a cliff, You are my shelter, and I find safety and renewed strength in You.

Amen.

We have this hope as an anchor for the soul, firm and secure.

HEBREWS 6:19

FATHER,

You are the Anchor of my soul.

It's easy for me, Lord, to drift from one opinion to another. But in this stormy time of trouble and doubt, my soul needs a safe harbor and a sturdy anchor. You are my Anchor, grounding me in the truth. You are my safe Harbor, surrounding me with Your love. I may be tossed by rough waters, but I am never lost, for You are my everlasting Hope.

Amen.

Be joyful in hope, patient in affliction, faithful in prayer.

ROMANS 12:12

FATHER,

It is a joy to place my hope in You.

Hope is hidden in the secret place in my heart. Though I have times when I doubt, in the deep center of my heart is a timeless trust. I trust You because I have come to know You—Your kindness, mercy, and love. Thank You, Lord, for revealing Yourself to me and thank You for placing Your Spirit deep within me so that I can always know that my hope in You is steady.

Amen.

•   •   •

When

I STRUGGLE WITH JEALOUSY . . .

A heart at peace gives life to the body, but envy rots the bones.

PROVERBS 14:30

FATHER,

You are the God of abundant blessings.

It's easy to lose sight of my own blessings when I am busy being envious of what others have. And it's easy to devalue who I am when I overvalue someone else because I am jealous. You show me that I am a woman of faith and have no need to be envious because my personal journey through life and my experience is unique. You are the God who blesses me with more than enough. Help me, Lord, to open my eyes and see a new reality.

Amen.

Let us not become conceited, provoking and envying each other.

GALATIANS 5:26

FATHER,

All glory belongs to You.

Thank You, Lord, for showing me that when I allow jealousy and pride to ruin my relationships, I am not glorifying You. Jealousy turns me into a competitive, whining, squabbling child, fighting for some kind of supposed position. Faith emphasizes our oneness in You and acknowledges that all glory belongs to You. Help me, Lord, to release my jealous feelings and choose to worship only You.

Amen.

•   •   •

When

I NEED JOY . . .

I delight greatly in the LORD; my soul rejoices in my God.

ISAIAH 61:10

FATHER,

You are the Joy of my heart.

When I am weary of the world, I come to You for renewal. In our time of intimate communion, You reveal Your love to me. Your voice speaks to my heart, telling me the secrets of the Kingdom. Thank You, Lord, for showing me that one of the delightful secrets of the Kingdom of God is the joy that bubbles up like a spring, renewing my heart and helping me find joy in You.

Amen.

When your words came, I ate them; they were my joy and my heart's delight, for I bear your name, O LORD God Almighty.

JEREMIAH 15:16

FATHER,

Your Word is a joy to me.

The cynicism of the world has gotten me down. Help me to come to Your Word and find renewed joy. Help me to discover a higher perspective that is not bound by time but flows from eternity. Show me eternal joys to light up my earthly life. And keep me always looking to You for the joy that comes only from Your salvation and Your presence in my life.

Amen.

> *Until now you have not asked for anything in my name. Ask and you will receive, and your joy will be complete.*

JOHN 16:24

FATHER,

You complete my joy.

Thank You for the gift of joy. I thank You for those days when the sun shines, all is right with the world, and happiness naturally springs up in my heart. But I thank You even more that Your joy is never dependent on outward circumstances, but that it is a mysterious inward gift that comes from Your work in my heart. I praise You, Lord, for Your constant goodness to me.

Amen.

*You have made known to me the path of life;
you will fill me with joy in your presence, with
eternal pleasures at your right hand.*

PSALM 16:11

FATHER,

Your joy is eternal.

During our life on earth, I have shed many tears and suffered many losses. But each time, You have reminded me that there will be no tears in my heavenly home—the one I will share with You for eternity. In that place, You have promised to wipe away the tears from my eyes and take away all pain. You will pour out Your joy on me. Today, as I struggle with a painful situation, help me to keep my eyes on Your promise of eternal life.

Amen.

•   •   •

When

I LONG TO SEE
JUSTICE . . .

He causes his sun to rise on the evil and the good, and sends rain on the righteous and the unrighteous.

MATTHEW 5:45

FATHER,

You are an impartial and generous God.

You are not a moral policeman, a do-good reformer, or a legalist. You do not hand me pat answers or offer easy platitudes in the face of my great need. Instead, You are a God who respects my right to choose—a right You Yourself provided—and who never manipulates me. Because You have been so patient and loving with me, I can trust You to bring justice to my situation.

Amen.

There is no difference between Jew and Gentile—the same Lord is Lord of all and richly blesses all who call on him.

ROMANS 10:12

FATHER,

You are Lord over all.

You do not label me an "outsider" or "insider," "winner" or "loser." You look, not at my outward appearance, but at my heart. Today, teach me to look on the heart and to see that You love each person, that You died for each one. When I see injustice, I remember that I do not know the end of the story. Only You know the full truth. I trust Your judgement, for You are Lord over all.

Amen.

"Whoever can be trusted with very little can also be trusted with much, and whoever is dishonest with very little will also be dishonest with much."

LUKE 16:10

FATHER,

You help me make right choices.

Justice begins with me. I must choose love over fear, kindness over cruelty, mercy over judgement. You empower me to discern the path of life over the path of death. As I prove myself a trustworthy servant, please, Lord, give me the strength to continue to make choices that are pleasing to You. Help me to make healing choices that honor You and show that I am Your child.

Amen.

Follow justice and justice alone, so that you may live and possess the land the LORD your God is giving you.

FATHER,

You give me discernment.

Sometimes the best cure for injustice is prevention. Help me to become sensitive to the motives of those around me—not judgmental, but aware, so that I will not be caught up in unjust situations like the one I find myself in today. And, Lord, help me to judge my own motives and offer them to You for purification so that I will not lead another person away from the paths of justice.

Amen.

*   *   *

When

I FEEL LONELY . . .

A friend loves at all times, and a brother is born for adversity.

PROVERBS 17:17

FATHER,

Your Son laid down His life for me.

If I were the only one who needed to be saved, You still would have sent Jesus and He still would have given His life for me. How can I be lonely when I have such a Friend? I praise You that no matter who my human friends may be, I have a Heavenly Friend who will never leave me or forsake me. As I focus my eyes on You, Lord, touch my heart and ease my loneliness with the fellowship of Your presence.

Amen.

May the Lord make your love increase and overflow for each other and for everyone else, just as ours does for you.

1 THESSALONIANS 3:12

FATHER,

Your love overflows to all.

Today it seems like no one cares what I'm going through. But I know that You care. You have compassion on me, and I share that compassion with others. When I am lonely, You urge me to look for others who are lonelier than I and reach out to them in Your name. As I focus on the needs of others, help my own loneliness to lose its grip on my life and release me to experience the love of others.

Amen.

·   ·   ·

When

I LONG TO BE LOVED . . .

Neither height nor depth, nor anything else in all creation, will be able to separate us from the love of God that is in Christ Jesus our Lord.

ROMANS 8:39

FATHER,

You love me with an immovable love.

A friend has forsaken me, but You will not forsake me. Because You love me and accept me, I do not have to be lonely, even when I am alone. Times of loneliness offer me a choice: Do I allow these feelings to rule my hours, or do I come to You for comfort and solace, resting in Your tender love for me? Help me, Lord, to make the right choice—the one that is pleasing to You.

Amen.

> *"As the Father has loved me, so have I loved you. Now remain in my love."*

JOHN 15:9

FATHER,

You love me.

You are a God of abundant love, a gentle Father who loves to answer His children's requests. You surround me with mercy and loving kindness. I am safe in Your love. On days like today when I am feeling unloved and unlovely, remind me that I have all the love I will ever need because I am loved by You.

Amen.

* * *

When

I NEED TO SHOW LOVE . . .

Love him as yourself, for you were aliens in Egypt.

LEVITICUS 19:34

FATHER,

You use my heart and hands to embrace the world.

Thank You, Lord, for sending me out to touch the world with Your love. In the process, I am reminded that Your love is always there for me, filling me up when I feel empty, healing me when I feel broken, giving my life value and meaning. Help me to remember that the love You have poured out on my life must be shared, and in the sharing, the reality of Your touch on my own life is revealed.

Amen.

Love the LORD your God with all your heart and
with all your soul and with all your strength.

DEUTERONOMY 6:5

FATHER,

I love You.

As a human being with needs and weaknesses, I do not love You perfectly. But I do love You, and I am learning how to perfect my love in You. I love You with my mind, delighting in Your wisdom. I love You with my heart, savoring our intimate communion. I love You with my strength, sharing Your love in practical ways with others. Lord, I love You. Teach me to love You better.

Amen.

> *May the Lord direct your hearts into God's love and Christ's perseverance.*

2 THESSALONIANS 3:5

FATHER,

You teach me how to love.

Every day is a fresh start. Every day is another opportunity to learn lessons in love. Love is patient, so I ask You to help me be patient in this difficult time. Love is kind, so I ask You to help me treat others with respect. Love is gentle, so I look to You to help me not to condemn myself or others for failure. You are Love, Lord. As I spend time in Your presence, show me what real love is.

Amen.

Remember those in prison as if you were their fellow prisoners, and those who are mistreated as if you yourselves were suffering.

FATHER,

You send people into my life to love.

Each person You bring into my life is a gift. You send me strangers to welcome, lonely people to embrace, and friends with whom to share life's journey. Increase my capacity for understanding and compassion, I pray. And send me those who are able to understand my pain and share my joy. And allow me to give love and receive it freely, just as You planned from the beginning.

Amen.

•　•　•

When

I NEED HELP IN MY MARRIAGE . . .

She sets about her work vigorously: her arms are strong for her tasks.

PROVERBS 31:17

FATHER,

You teach me to love in practical ways.

Help me, Lord, to create a safe place for love to grow. Instead of expecting marriage to be an endless date, help me to make it an opportunity to express love through gentle service. As I reach out to my husband, give me the discernment to understand his needs and be a blessing in his life. Each day, teach me new ways to express my love to him.

Amen.

Be completely humble and gentle; be patient,
bearing with one another in love.

EPHESIANS 4:2

FATHER,

You help me see my mate with loving eyes.

It is easy to think that because we have lived together for such a long time that we know each other. But I know that my husband and I are complex beings, changing in relationship to the world, each other, and ourselves. I ask that You would give me eyes to see my mate with love and understanding and to be aware of that which I have taken for granted. Thank You for the gifts of awareness and appreciation.

Amen.

•   •   •

When

I NEED MERCY . . .

The LORD has heard my cry for mercy; the LORD accepts my prayer.

PSALM 6:9

FATHER,

Your mercies are new every morning.

Summer and winter, spring and autumn, season after season You renew Your mercy and compassion in my life. As the seasons change, so I change. But You never change. You are merciful to me, even when I am wrong. Like the father of the prodigal son, You run to meet me. You are great in mercy, Lord, but I am not. Help me to be merciful to myself, forgiving myself so that I do not become weighted down with self-pity.

Amen.

Carry each other's burdens, and in this way you will fulfill the law of Christ.

GALATIANS 6:2

FATHER,

You teach me mercy.

You are merciful to me, Lord. You use my relationships to teach me the gentle lessons of mercy's generous gifts. You use my circumstances to teach me to live a merciful life. But even now, my nature cries out for revenge rather than love and compassion. Give me a new heart—one that is willing to carry the burdens of others, giving mercy in the same measure that I have received mercy from You.

Amen.

•   •   •

When

I NEED PATIENCE . . .

The end of a matter is better than its beginning, and patience is better than pride.

ECCLESIASTES 7:8

FATHER,

You help me become more patient.

You know how impatient I can be. I want solutions to my problems and resolutions to my dilemmas right now—right away. Teach me, Lord, to learn the lessons of the patient farmer waiting for his field to grow. As I wait for You to help me sort out my circumstances, place in me a patient and hopeful heart—a heart that is pleasing to You.

Amen.

You need to persevere so that when you have done the will of God, you will receive what he has promised.

HEBREWS 10:36

FATHER,

You reward the patient heart.

In this time of stress and anxiety, I am impatient. I want answers, and I want them right now. Like a frustrated child, I begin to whine. You are a gentle Father who loves me even when I am being tiresome. Forgive me, Lord, for my childishness. Help me to cast all my anxieties on You and rest in Your love, believing that one day patience will have its reward.

Amen.

See how the farmer waits for the land to yield its valuable crop and how patient he is for the autumn and spring rains.

JAMES 5:7

FATHER,

I wait patiently for You.

Thank You for helping me wait for the right timing. I understand that there is a perfect timing for me. You are orchestrating wonderful outcomes behind the curtain of time's mystery. In all my affairs, there is a season, and I allow Your patience to flow into my life. Help me, Lord, to release my controlling need to know and to rest patiently in the mystery of Your will, waiting for the right time.

Amen.

> *Be still before the LORD and wait patiently for him; do not fret when men . . . carry out their wicked schemes.*

FATHER,

I quietly trust You.

The world is a noisy place, filled with people trying to push forward their own agendas. No one has time to wait—they demand instant answers and immediate action. But I can see that the most worthwhile things in life are a product of time and patience. Help me discern when action is needed and when to sit back and wait for the right timing. Help me to wait patiently for the full fruition of Your plan.

Amen.

*   *   *

When

I NEED PEACE . . .

*If only you had paid attention to my commands,
your peace would have been like a river, your
righteousness like the waves of the sea.*

ISAIAH 48:18

FATHER,

You give me peace like a river.

A river flows on and on. Even in this drought, when I feel parched by life's trials, the river of life still flows from Your throne. It cleanses and heals the land, providing water for life. So, too, does Your peace flow like a river through me. Like a green tree planted by streams of living water, I find my peace in You. Help me, Lord, never to wander away from the peaceful waters of Your Spirit.

Amen.

Let the peace of Christ rule in your hearts, since as members of one body you were called to peace.

COLOSSIANS 3:15

FATHER,

You call me to be a peacemaker.

Petty arguments, grudges, gossip, anger, and jealousy—all of these create a war in my heart. How easy it is to take up weapons against other people, putting pride before compassion. Thank You, Lord, for commanding me to disarm, to help the peaceable kingdom come. As I make my peace with You, bring inner peace to all my relationships. Give me a peaceful heart with which to conquer the world with love.

Amen.

I will lie down and sleep in peace, for you alone, O LORD, make me dwell in safety.

PSALM 4:8

FATHER,

Tonight I rest in Your love.

My heart has been troubled today. I have felt frustrated and upset. There has been static in the atmosphere—the day has been turbulent. Now, at the end of this day, I bring my troubles to You. I meditate on Your promises and take time to quiet my spirit. Now I will go to sleep, knowing that You watch through the night and will bring new mercies in the morning.

Amen.

Glory to God in the highest, and on earth peace to men on whom his favor rests.

LUKE 2:14

FATHER,

You will bring peace to the earth.

The world is at war with itself. Every day in newspapers and on television I see scenes of strife. Even in my own home and workplace, I struggle to get along with others. Peace is Your miracle. It begins with transformed hearts. In Your plan, the fullness of time will bring peace to the entire world. Until that time, help me to appreciate Your promises of peace and joy.

Amen.

•   •   •

When

I STRUGGLE WITH PRIDE . . .

Humble yourselves before the Lord, and he will lift you up.

JAMES 4:10

FATHER,

I trust You with my reputation.

It is so easy for me to get caught up in the game of jockeying for position: I need to be on that committee. I want to hobnob with the important people. I want to be powerful and admired. But when I try to make these things happen, I get hurt and so do others. Teach me, Lord, to trust You with my reputation and with the desires of my heart. I let go of my agendas to make room for Your surprises.

Amen.

> *The greatest among you should be like the youngest, and the one who rules like the one who serves.*

LUKE 22:26

FATHER,

You teach me graceful humility.

It's tempting to push my way to first place and step on people to get ahead. But You have taught me that such a path will cause me to lose in the long run, even if I achieve my objectives in the short run. Your Kingdom is run on a different set of standards. People who walk in graceful humility are praised. Your Son came as a servant. Teach me, Lord, to lay aside pride and live Your way.

Amen.

• • •

When

I NEED HELP WITH MY PRIORITIES . . .

Do not conform any longer to the pattern of this world, but be transformed by the renewing of your mind.

ROMANS 12:2

FATHER,

I seek Your wisdom.

My greatest priority is to do Your will on earth as it is done in heaven. You show me in the Scripture that Your ways are not my ways and that Your kingdom is not run the way the kingdoms of the earth are run. Set my mind, Lord, to learn Your ways and my heart to follow Your paths. Remind me every day that following You is my greatest priority.

Amen.

Do not boast about tomorrow, for you do not know what a day may bring forth.

PROVERBS 27:1

FATHER,

I depend on Your wisdom and guidance.

I make my plans and do the best I can, but I cannot plan for every contingency. In the end, it is character as much as strength that counts in any situation. I seek Your wisdom and ask You to help me choose lasting priorities. Show me where I need to improve even as You comfort me with Your love. Guide me, Lord, for I look to You.

Amen.

*I guide you in the way of wisdom and lead
you along straight paths.*

PROVERBS 4:11

FATHER,

You help me to live wisely.

It's easy to identify the obvious mistakes like addiction
and abuse. But there is also a way which seems right in
our eyes but leads to destruction as surely as drugs and
weapons. Thank You, Lord, for arranging my priorities
for the highest good, for correcting me when I need to
change my course. I am not alone. You walk beside me,
guiding me away from danger.

Amen.

> *Wisdom is supreme; therefore get wisdom.*
> *Though it costs all you have, get understanding.*

PROVERBS 4:7

FATHER,

You are my source of all wisdom.

Sometimes I feel very sure of myself, filled with self-confidence. But today, I see my own foolishness and run to You for the wisdom and understanding I lack. Thank You, Lord, for giving Your wisdom freely when I ask for it. Thank You for giving it without scolding or chiding me. Without You, I would come to nothing. But with You, I can achieve all You have planned for me.

Amen.

*   *   *

When

I NEED PROTECTION . . .

---

*The angel of the LORD encamps around those
who fear him, and he delivers them.*

PSALM 34:7

FATHER,

You are my Protector.

When I am in need of protection, You are there. You send Your angels to keep guard around me. You guide me through dangerous territory and lead me on a safe path. Though trouble surrounds me, You show me the way of escape. You are more powerful than all my adversaries, and You protect me. Thank You, Lord, for watching over me and keeping me safe.

Amen.

> *As the mountains surround Jerusalem, so the* LORD *surrounds his people both now and forevermore.*

PSALM 125:2

FATHER,

I am surrounded by Your love.

I am not alone in any situation. You are always present, surrounding me with Your love. Like a mighty fortress, this wall of love protects me from the arrows of the enemy. Yet I am never boxed in or coerced, for Your love sets me free. Because of Your love, I dare to be who I am and reach out to a world in need. Help me, Lord, to trust in You more and more each day.

Amen.

•   •   •

When

I NEED HELP WITH RELATIONSHIPS . . .

Therefore let us stop passing judgment on one another.

ROMANS 14:13

FATHER,

You enable me to look at others with compassion.

It is easy to magnify the faults of others and to take offense or hold a grudge. It is easy to complain about how I am being mistreated or how another person is letting You down. Help me, Lord, to see beyond my own judgments and see that person as You see him or her. Teach me to treat others with compassion rather than focusing on my own correctness.

Amen.

> *Have we not all one Father? Did not one*
> *God create us? Why do we profane the*
> *covenant of our fathers by breaking faith with*
> *one another?*

MALACHI 2:10

FATHER,

You teach me believe for the best in others.

It is too easy to let my tongue slip. A little gossip here, a snide comment there—suddenly I find myself in the quicksand of self-righteousness. Lord, teach me to close my mouth, open my eyes, and see Your work in the people I have been belittling. Teach me to keep faith with Your children and believe for the best in them. Thank You for Your patience and forgiveness in my own life.

Amen.

My command is this: Love each other as I have loved you.

JOHN 15:12

FATHER,

You help me love others.

You are constantly teaching me about Your love through the relationships in my life. I learn about patience from those who frustrate and anger me. I learn about compassion from those who hurt and wrong me. I learn about love from those who have loved me faithfully through the years despite my faults. Lord, I thank You for using my relationships to make me a better person—a person who is pleasing to You.

Amen.

> *Now that you have purified yourselves by obeying the truth so that you have sincere love for your brothers, love one another deeply, from the heart.*
>
> 1 PETER 1:22

FATHER,

I love more deeply because You have healed me.

One of the delights of being Your child is the gift of lasting love—a love that looks beyond the surface to the hidden treasures beneath. Thank You, Lord, for sending Your Spirit to gently teach and heal me. Your love gives me the courage to love others. Thank You, Father, for the relationships You have brought into my life and especially for allowing me to have a relationship with You.

Amen.

•　　•　　•

When

I NEED RESTORATION . . .

*The LORD will sustain him on his sickbed and
restore him from his bed of illness.*

PSALM 41:3

FATHER,

You restore my body and my spirit.

Thank You, Lord, for sustaining me with Your love and
kindness. I rest and am restored in Your presence as You
open Your loving arms to me. Teach me to receive all You
wish to give me—to stand still as You refill me and
restore me to newness of life in my body, my soul, and
my spirit. Thank You for all Your goodness to me and the
way You watch over me.

Amen.

They will rebuild the ancient ruins and restore the places long devastated; they will renew the ruined cities that have been devastated for generations.

ISAIAH 61:4

FATHER,

You are the God who makes me whole.

Like the ancient cities that the children of Israel rebuilt time and again, You restore my ruins. Today, I come to You once more, asking for the touch of Your healing hand on my life. I need to know the miracle of Your forgiveness and call upon Your promise to help me rebuild what my foolishness has torn down. Thank You, Lord, for Your constant love and grace.

Amen.

•   •   •

When

I FEEL SHAME . . .

Those who look to him are radiant; their faces are never covered with shame.

PSALM 34:5

FATHER,

You take away my shame.

No matter how hard I try, Lord, I continue to go astray, allowing my human nature to rule my thoughts and actions. And each time I do, I feel the sting of guilt and shame. Thank You for Your promise that Your forgiveness covers every sin as long as I am faithful to confess it to You. Today, I need Your cleansing touch once again. Wash away my sin and shame, and make me fit to be in Your presence once more.

Amen.

Remove from me scorn and contempt, for I keep your statutes.

PSALM 119: 22

FATHER,

I find refuge in You.

Though I have confessed my sin to You, Lord, my shame lingers in the eyes of those I have wronged. Show me how to make restitution if that is possible. Lay upon me a burden of prayer for those who continue to carry the weight of my poor choices and selfish deeds. And help me to walk in the light of Your forgiveness, despite how others may feel. My sin was real and my shame was deserved, but You have paid my debt.

Amen.

•   •   •

When

I NEED STABILITY . . .

My flesh and my heart may fail, but God is the strength of my heart and my portion forever.

PSALM 73:26

FATHER,

You are my Strength and my Salvation.

During this time of trouble and chaos, I depend on You. I find stability in my faith. My current situation may be uncertain, but Your love is as certain as the dawn. When doubt overwhelms me, I meditate on Your Word. No matter how unstable my world seems to be, You are my sure Foundation. Thank You, Lord, for Your promise to walk beside me throughout my journey, lifting me up when I'm weak and keeping my feet steady on the path. *Amen.*

You broaden the path beneath me, so that my ankles do not turn.

FATHER,

You lead me safely.

Today I have encountered a rocky place in my journey through life. Thank You for Your promise to lead me one step at a time, across difficult and dangerous terrain. Because I know that You are a kind Shepherd, I will trust You to guide my feet around this obstacle and on to green pastures where I can find rest and restoration for my soul.

Amen.

•   •   •

When

I NEED STRENGTH . . .

I love you, O LORD, my strength.

FATHER,

You are my Strength.

Whenever I need it, I know that Your strength is available to me. It is always there to empower me to do the right thing, to continue to fight the good fight of faith. I come to You right now, in need. Thank You, Lord, for hearing me and filling me with supernatural power to do what I must do. Thank You for giving me all I need to accomplish Your plan for my life.

Amen.

My help comes from the LORD, the Maker of heaven and earth.

PSALM 121:2

FATHER,

My help and strength come from You.

I have done all that I can, Lord. Now I come to You with a humble heart, asking You to step in and rescue me from this circumstance in my life. I lay myself and my concerns at Your feet, for You are my Hope and my Salvation. Though I am weak, You are strong. You are glorified even in the weakness of Your children, for You love to give us what we need. You are my Helper, and You renew my strength.

Amen.

The foolishness of God is wiser than man's wisdom, and the weakness of God is stronger than man's strength.

1 CORINTHIANS 1:25

FATHER,

You are the Source of real strength.

I know that I cannot place my security in the strength of armies and navies. They may seem invincible, able to conquer the world, and yet, they are nothing compared to You. Though they wield great power, they have no sway over the human heart. Their fortunes change day to day and are subject to changing circumstances and the whims of man. I will place my trust in You, Lord, and look to You for my strength and security.

Amen.

I can do everything through him who gives me strength.

PHILIPPIANS 4:13

FATHER,

You give me abundant strength.

You know, Lord, that I want to do what is right. My heart cries out for it. And yet, I simply cannot accomplish it in my own strength. I find myself distracted by circumstances, swayed by the opinions of others, sidetracked by personal needs and concerns. I need Your strength. Open my heart to receive what I need from Your hand this day.

Amen.

• • •

> *Therefore we do not lose heart. Though outwardly we are wasting away, yet inwardly we are being renewed day by day.*

2 CORINTHIANS 4:16

FATHER,

I find renewal in You.

I am tired and stressed. Therefore, I come to You for new strength. Every morning Your mercies are fresh, and every night I rest in Your care. Though my day may frazzle me, when I take time to be with You I am refreshed and renewed. You calm the storms of my life, and I find peace in Your presence. Thank You, Lord, for pouring out Your grace on my life again today.

Amen.

Let the peace of Christ rule in your hearts.

COLOSSIANS 3:15

FATHER,

You are my Peace.

This was a stressful day. It was frustrating, aggravating, and irritating. Though I know it was a day that You have made, I'm glad it's over. Tonight I come to You asking for peace—and knowing that even before I ask, You have touched my heart with forgiving mercy. Melt away my anxiety and restore me. Help me to wake tomorrow ready to live a victorious life once more.

Amen.

> *I said, "Oh, that I had the wings of a dove! I would fly away and be at rest—I would flee far away and stay in the desert."*

PSALM 55:6-7

FATHER,

You lead me to a quiet place of retreat.

Sometimes, Lord, I wish I could fly away. Though the desert was a favorite place for saints and prophets to find You, I personally prefer some deserted tropical beach. Since I can't have the luxury of a long vacation from my life, I come to You right now for a mini-retreat—a cup of tea and the Good Book. Thank You for small islands of refreshment in my day.

Amen.

Unless the LORD builds the house, its builders labor in vain.

PSALM 127:1

FATHER,

You make all things work for good.

I've discovered something interesting in my walk with You. Things go better when You are in control. It's funny how stressed out I get when I am trying to control everything. I micromanage the process, thinking I know the best way to accomplish my goals. I release control of this situation right now and allow You to work things out in my life and take this stressful burden from me.

Amen.

•   •   •

When

I LONG TO SUCCEED . . .

Many are the plans in a man's heart, but it is the LORD's purpose that prevails.

PROVERBS 19:21

FATHER,

You lead me to true success.

Oh Lord, You know that all my life I've had a difficult time defining success. When I was in high school, I thought it was popularity. As an adult my definition of success changed, but it still contained elements of selfishness and status. Thank You for teaching me that true success has nothing much to do with earthly possessions, status, or achievement. It has to do with living a life that is pleasing to You. When I go astray, please bring me back to the truth.

Amen.

Let us not become weary in doing good, for at the proper time we will reap a harvest if we do not give up.

FATHER,

You help me keep on keeping on.

I know, Lord, that success is not an instant thing. And yet, I catch myself looking, longing, even expecting to find that one magical thing that will put me over the top and make me feel successful. Thank You for reminding me that true success is made up of the collective acts of a life lived in Your will. I'm sure to get off track from time to time. Thank You for pointing me back to those things that will last forever.

Amen.

*If the ax is dull and its edge unsharpened, more
strength is needed but skill will bring success.*

FATHER,

You are all I really need.

O Lord, there are so many things out there that
promise success: books, speakers, and classes that
promise me a successful outcome to my endeavors.
Thank You for helping me to cut through the hype and
take those things that help me to carry out Your vision for
my life. And thank You for reminding me that all You ask
is that I work hard and do my best for You.

Amen.

May the favor of the Lord our God rest upon us; establish the work of our hands for us.

PSALM 90:17

FATHER,

You bless my work.

Thank You for teaching me that I can take pride in my work because I do it for You. That keeps me working to faithfully do what needs to be done to the best of my ability. Today, I know that I've done a good job and even though no one else seems to have noticed, I will not allow myself to become frustrated or discouraged because I know You noticed and You are pleased with me.

Amen.

* * *

When

I DON'T UNDERSTAND SUFFERING . . .

Just as the sufferings of Christ flow over into our lives, so also through Christ our comfort overflows.

2 CORINTHIANS 1:5

FATHER,

You comfort me in my suffering.

I realize that the mystery of suffering, Lord, cannot always be understood. It must be embraced by faith. I also know that You understand my suffering because You have suffered on my behalf. Father, I thank You for comfort in times of sorrow. Though I do not understand with my mind, my heart knows You are with me and You will work all things for good according to Your will.

Amen.

He has not despised or disdained the suffering of the afflicted one; he has not hidden his face from him but has listened to his cry for help.

PSALM 22:24

FATHER,

You care about my suffering.

You do not dismiss or despise my suffering. You care about the hardship and sorrow found in the world. I believe that, Lord, even though I don't see it now. The Psalms say that You keep all my tears in a bottle, that every hair on my head is numbered. In this time of sorrow, it is not answers that count but Your compassionate presence that heals me.

Amen.

•   •   •

When

I Struggle with Temptation . . .

No temptation has seized you except what is common to man. And God is faithful; he will not let you be tempted beyond what you can bear.

1 Corinthians 10:13

FATHER,

You provide a way out of temptation.

I can't say, "The devil made me do it." No, You have given me the priceless gift of free will, and I will not cheapen that gift by allowing another to control me. But I do fall into temptation, and sometimes I feel so weak. Help me to make the right choice—to follow You rather than my greedy self-will. And thank You for Your promise that You will always provide a way for me to escape temptation. All I need to do is use it.

Amen.

My son, if sinners entice you, do not give in to them.

PROVERBS 1:10

FATHER,

You give me discernment.

Today, Lord, someone made me an offer I didn't want to refuse, even though I knew it would not be pleasing to You. Temptation can be attractive, wrapped up in promises of instant gratification and easy riches. You give me the discernment to know the difference between a genuine opportunity and a get-rich-quick scheme. Thank You for helping me choose the highest good for all concerned rather than the easy way out.

Amen.

• • •

When

I AM THANKFUL . . .

Enter his gates with thanksgiving and his courts with praise; give thanks to him and praise his name.

PSALM 100:4

FATHER,

I thank You.

My heart is overflowing with gratitude. You have blessed me in so many ways, and I am anxious to praise you wherever I go. Hymns of thanksgiving rise up in my heart, and I cannot keep from speaking them out loud. I find myself telling others how much You mean to me—how much You have brought to my life. Thank You, Lord, for Your goodness, and receive my praise today.

Amen.

> *Let the peace of Christ rule in your hearts,*
> *since as members of one body you were called*
> *to peace. And be thankful.*

COLOSSIANS 3:15

FATHER,

You give me the gift of life.

From my first breath to my last, You surround me with Your love and care. I praise You for the goodness of this earthly life. I thank You for the gift of breath and health and loved ones and worthwhile work to do. I thank You for my heavenly home, the place where I will one day see You face to face. I thank You for life.

Amen.

O Lord, open my lips, and my mouth will declare your praise.

PSALM 51:15

FATHER,

I praise You in all circumstances.

You are Lord over all, and I thank You for Your presence in each circumstance of my life. When I am happy, I praise You for the joy of living. When I am sad, I thank You for Your loving care. When I am worried, You ask me to set aside my fears and take time to give You the honor and glory. I speak and sing freely in Your presence in every circumstance because Your love has given me a song to sing.

Amen.

Through Jesus, therefore, let us continually offer to God a sacrifice of praise—the fruit of lips that confess his name.

HEBREWS 13:15

FATHER,

You are worthy to be praised.

What a wonderful work You have done in my life. And what an incredible salvation You have wrought for the earth. You are the great Creator who has made the natural world to be so beautiful. You are the compassionate Redeemer who has saved us from our sin. You are the loving Father who holds the whole world in His hands. You are worthy to be praised. What an honor it is to worship You.

Amen.

•   •   •

When

I Am Facing a Tragedy . . .

"My grace is sufficient for you, for my power is made perfect in weakness."

---

2 Corinthians 12:9

FATHER,

You are strong when I am weak.

O Lord, I feel so helpless in the face of this tragedy. Events are out of my hands and I have no control over what has happened. Even though I know better, life seems meaningless, as if there is no reason or purpose to the events that have occurred. Lord, I throw myself on You today. I deed to You my will, my emotions, my soul. Help me I pray. I look to You for the strength I need to go on.

Amen.

I consider that our present sufferings are not worth comparing with the glory that will be revealed in us.

ROMANS 8:18

FATHER,

Your Kingdom come, Your will be done.

Today I find no comfort in this life; I find comfort in Your promises only. In the midst of the darkness that has come into my life, give me a glimpse of future glory. Give me the strength and the courage to seek Your will even now and to allow You to find some good in my present circumstances. I have no faith, no strength, no will of my own. I am completely dependent on You for my very breath. Lift me up, Lord, I pray.

Amen.

*   *   *

When

I LONG FOR THE TRUTH . . .

This is what we speak, not in words taught us by human wisdom but in words taught by the Spirit, expressing spiritual truths in spiritual words.

1 CORINTHIANS 2:13

FATHER,

You show me the truth.

Thank You, Lord, for revealing truth to me in ways that I can understand. You compensate for my uncertainty by couching it in things that I know and can relate to. I ask You to always keep me connected to those things that are right and true. Continue to open my heart to see, not what my selfish will wants to see, but the realities of eternity.

Amen.

When he, the Spirit of truth, comes, he will guide you into all truth.

JOHN 16:13

FATHER,

You help me understand the truth.

O Lord, I know so much of the truth in my head, but I realize that it must be translated to my heart. I don't want to be one of those people who can quote the Bible and build a good argument, yet lacks the embodiment of the truth in my life. No matter how good the words sound, it is nothing but noise unless love leads the way. Help me understand and apply truth so it reaches my heart.

Amen.

•   •   •

When

I Need Help In My Work . . .

If you are willing and obedient, you will eat the best from the land.

ISAIAH 1:19

FATHER,

You reward obedience and diligence.

You reward good work, and a job well done is its own reward. O Lord, help me to remember that. Help me to concern myself with building character in my life rather than glorying in the surface results. Teach me not to waste opportunities but to value those contributions You allow me to make to the Kingdom. And I promise to do all I can to use my time wisely and give my best to my work. Thank You for the blessing of work.

Amen.

Let your light shine before men, that they may see your good deeds and praise your Father in heaven.

MATTHEW 5:16

FATHER.

Work faithfully done honors You.

Help me to honor You today by giving my best effort to my work and seeing each job through to the end. In this way, I wish to be a witness to those I work with of Your grace and love in my life. You have given me so much that I cannot hesitate to give back all that I can. Show me new ways in which to use the opportunities You give me. May my work honor You all the days of my life.

Amen.

Serve wholeheartedly, as if you were serving the Lord, not men.

EPHESIANS 6: 7

FATHER,

I do my best work for You because I love You.

O Lord, You are the Source of all the gifts and talents in my life. I'm overwhelmed by the confidence that You have shown in me, and I want to thank You by doing my very best for You. It is work done in love—the gift of a grateful heart devoted to You and Your purposes. Thank You, Lord, for all You have done. Give me the grace to greet each task with a heart of love and devotion for You. *Amen.*

The wicked man earns deceptive wages, but he who sows righteousness reaps a sure reward.

PROVERBS 11:18

FATHER,

You reward worthy work.

Today I feel overworked and underpaid. I read about an executive who mismanaged funds and got away with a small fortune. Even though I know that honest work is pleasing in Your eyes, it's easy to be frustrated by those who do what they should not and prosper while I work so hard just to make ends meet. Help me to remember that Your rewards extend beyond mere money. I submit my work to You and thank You for the opportunity to please You in it.

Amen.

＊　　＊　　＊

I AM WORRIED . . .

Commit your way to the LORD; trust in him and he will do this.

PSALM 37:5

FATHER,

I commit my worries to You.

You call me to faith, not fear. You have given me many promises. Now in this time of doubt and struggle, I ask for the grace to meditate on Your promises instead of chewing over my worries. Watch over me, Lord. Don't allow me to waste my energies rehearsing worst case scenarios in my mind. Help me instead to remember all the times You have helped me. Teach me once again to trust You with my problems and let You do the worrying.

Amen.

You will keep in perfect peace him whose mind is steadfast, because he trusts in you.

ISAIAH 26:3

FATHER,

You give me peace.

Lord, worry and anxiety are stressing me out, making my life miserable and leaving me tired and cranky. Help me to leave my cares at Your feet, trusting You to show me what I need to do, if anything, to change the situation. As I let go, I ask You to work out the details and orchestrate what I cannot see or control in this situation. I promise to keep my mind stayed on You, so that Your perfect peace can flood my heart and mind.

Amen.

•   •   •

When

I NEED WISDOM . . .

How many are your works, O LORD! In wisdom you made them all; the earth is full of your creatures.

PSALM 104:24

FATHER,

I find lessons of wisdom in Your creation.

Thank You, Lord, for the beautiful world You have created. Today I found myself distracted and unsettled, but as I walked along the road taking in the wonders around me, I gained new perspective. I looked at the leaves on the trees and marveled at the changing seasons. I plucked a wild flower and praised You for the startling detail You place in everything You have created. The birds reminded me that I also have a song to sing. Thank You for the beauty and wisdom You have placed in the world. *Amen.*

Blessed is the man who finds wisdom, the man who gains understanding.

FATHER,

I seek Your wisdom.

The world shouts at me, demanding that I buy into its agendas. Noisy advertisements distract me and try to manipulate me with fear. It seems that everyone has something to sell. Tonight, I turned off the TV, and now I am waiting in this quiet place, where You can help me to regain perspective—a place where Your wisdom and truth can reign and rule. Thank You for wisdom from above.

Amen.

Better to meet a bear robbed of her cubs than a fool in his folly.

FATHER,

You give me common sense.

Thank You, Lord, for giving me discernment so that I do not get caught up in foolish schemes or time-wasting crises. Thank You for protecting me from the follies of my own wishful thinking and grandiose imaginations. You are good to clear those out of the path so that I can follow the legitimate dreams You have placed in my heart and mind. I am grateful for Your presence in my life.

Amen.

190 • Everyday Prayers for Everyday Cares for Women

> *Oh, the depth of the riches of the wisdom and knowledge of God! How unsearchable his judgments, and his paths beyond tracing out!*
>
> ROMANS 11:33

FATHER,

Your wisdom is great and wonderful.

Lord, thank You for reminding me that I don't have all the answers, that I am a mere child in my understanding. And thank You for urging me to seek out Your wisdom, which is much greater and more mysterious than I can ever fathom. Though Your ways are above my ways, still You love to share Your wisdom with me. And I'm grateful. My ways can only leave me disappointed and unfulfilled, but Your ways will lead me to a truly happy life.

Amen.

* * *

Additional copies of this book and other
titles from Honor Books
are available from your local bookstore.

Everyday Prayers for Everyday Cares
Everyday Prayers for Everyday Cares for Parents
Everyday Prayers for Everyday Cares for Mothers

If you have enjoyed this book,
or if it has impacted your life,
we would like to hear from you.

Please contact us at:

Honor Books

Department E

P.O. Box 55388

Tulsa, Oklahoma 74155

Or by e-mail at *info@honorbooks.com*